# Snippets Of Kim

Kim Arnott

BookLeaf
Publishing

India | USA | UK

Presentation by *BookLeaf Publishing*

Web: www.bookleafpub.com

E-mail: info@bookleafpub.com

ISBN: 978-93-5744-927-4

First edition 2022

# DEDICATION

To mum and dad They made me who I am

To my boy's for being mirrors

I learn from them so much

# ACKNOWLEDGEMENT

To all my boy's. Big and Small
I love you all

# PREFACE

I never quite know where my poetry is going;
but I do enjoy the journey

# The City

I am the City
I am Shades of grey
Shades of grey; by light of day
So many shoes; walk my way
Walk my way; all through the day
But then comes night; neon bright
Neon bright in the night
I am the city
I am champagne I am champagne
But when daylight; exposes me again
I turn once more; to shades of grey
Shades of grey; city by day
Neon bright; City by night
I am the  City
Kim Arnott

# Pink Toes

Pink Toes and Satin bows
Paper dolls; with paper clothes
Yesterday is all I know
Tomorrow comes; then it goes

Put it in the memory box
Where everything I knew; was lost
Nothing is quite as it seems
Still I have some hope; some dreams

Tomorrow comes; then it goes
Paper dolls with paper clothes
Almost real; Almost themed
It never was quite what it seemed

It's almost gone; yet not quite there
The real stories; we can share
I had pink toes and satin bows
And paper dolls; with paper clothes

I'm not made of paper; I am real
I can be touched: I can feel
Tomorrow's here; but then it goes
Towards whichever path I chose
Kim Arnott

# Dear Drunk Driver

Dear Drunk Driver
I am talking to you
Why do you let alcohol
Control all; that you do
You know; that we love you
I need you alive
Yet you still continue; to drink when you drive

Dear Drunk Driver
Please; think about this
Your children are young yet
Just think; what you will miss
You may say that you love us
That seems like such a lie
Dear Drunk Driver
I am asking you why

Dear Drunk Driver
I am asking you why
You say: That is the way you live
It is your choice how you die
Yet the blood is on your hands
On your hands; alone
If that head on your dashboard
Is'nt your own
Kim Arnott

# I Carried You

I carried you until you could stand
Then I walked beside you; I held your hand
As you grew stronger everyday
I walked with you to guide your way

Then one day as it should be
You don't hold my hand; you won't walk with me
And so I walk just steps behind
To make sure your way you find

Then one day when you could run
A journey of your own had begun
So often you looked back to see
If the one with you is me

Then a day comes when it's not enough to walk or run
You have to fly; my job is done
As you go to places I will never see
I know this is as it should be
Kim Arnott

# Meeting my son

I made a person today
No I did really. Yes me!
He has eyes like an owl
His skin is so soft and fuzzy
It's like holding a peach
And his head moves so randomly
When he looks up at me
His stare is so intent
It fills me right up I feel so content
Just to sit here and hold him
Though it seems that he holds me
In his spell
I made a person today
But I think that actually
He made me
Kim Arnott

# Jigsaw

Our life is a jigsaw
Where the pieces just don't fit
I have studied them; I have turned them
But I can't connect all the bits
There are interlocking boarders
I've linked pieces of the sky
But the pieces that form us
Seem to be missing; Or awry
I am stuggling  to see the picture
Though it was once so easy to do
But no  matter how hard I try
I can't see me and you
Kim Arnott

# Devoured by Wolves

Did your hopes and your dreams
Get devoured by wolves
Did you lose each other
Searching for yourselves
Did your tears turn into a storm
Did you play it so cool
That you could never feel warmth
Have you tried so hard to connect
Yet you are still alone
Did it ever feel real
Maybe you will never know
Standing on a ledge; shouting out hello
Did somebody answer you
Or was it just an echo
Your own voice calling back to you
Kim Arnott

# Red Balloon

If I were a red balloon
Then I could touch the sky
I would be at every party
Putting twinkles into eye's
But if I were a red balloon
You couldn't hold onto me
I could only be yours; at intervals
You would have to set me free

If I were a brown pebble
That you found upon a beach
You could put me in your pocket
Always keeping me in reach
A Pebble  it is solid; in your hands I would be
warm
I would always travel with you
For you would be my home

In my heart I am a pebble
Yet my mind is a red balloon
I long to party and to fly away
But I want to belong to you
So I can't just be a pebble; nor a red balloon
But if you can let me fly away
I will want to come home soon
Kim Arnott

# The Onion

There are many beautiful flowers in this world
Me. I am an onion
Most of me is out of sight
But if you peel back one layer
You will find another one; add infinitum
And yet not the same
I am not a flower; I am not visibly perfect
You will not write poems about me
Who writes poems about an onion
An ode to an onion would be a comedy
I am not an emblem inspiring loyalty
I will never change the world
An onion on a lapel?
It would hardly inspire hope or tears
But if you should try to cut through my layers
You may cry

# Evolving

I am transparent
I am there; yet I am not
I am a jelly fish
Floating in an ocean
Invisible yet visible

I appear
I am your whole world
A lamb; warm blooded and soft
You want to protect me
Protected I transform

I am a lizard
I need you; but I don't
I sit on a rock; sunning myself
Watching; Seeing; learning; frozen in a pose

Now you see me; I frolic just for fun
I am a purring; pleasing ; teasing; kitten
casually I brush-against your leg
Attentive under your attention

I change again, over here; look at me
I am no longer coy
I swim round in my bowl; attention seeking

A dizzy glorious goldfish; you watch entranced

Now I become a Doberman
Sitting on your doorstep;Waiting for a pat
Floppy; huge eyes; loyal
Content to wait for you

But you looked away
I become a snapping snarling redhead
A dingo protecting her young
You could do no wrong now you
 can do nothing right

Possessed by love I have become
A slithering snake laying in wait
On my belly ready to strike
At all who would hurt what I created

I shed my skin again and rise up
A Phoenix; flying high; heading for the sun
I am not yet done; I no longer see you
I have someplace else to belong

So I ascend; then descend one last time
I have become an eagle
Powerful; purposeful; alone
I have my own journey now; I fly home
Kim Arnott

# Do lives Matter?

Can we say that human lives matter?
We come and we go
In the scheme of the universe
We are the blink of an eye
Time is subjective; as marked by the sky
Age is recorded by people
As birthdays; in years
It is quantitive; not quality
What  then makes a good life;?
 if you work all your life
In a job that you hate
To put food on the table
Are you happier than a slave?
You could be a victim of war or of crime
You could be a victim of parents who
don't ' have the time
You could live in a palace or live in a tent
And not be in good health
You could never know friends
Because of personality or wealth
Maybe your dying; or live day to day
You may not feel safe;To relax; sleep or play
But who you are on the inside
Is what you must live with; or fight
Should our lives matter above others?

Who is wrong; who is right
For our thoughts and our feelings
Are not wrong; or right
Our people they matter
They are our hearts and our souls
What we believe in
What makes us whole
Could we just live together?
 show love;Show respect
All lives  they should matter
So we can live; no regrets
Kim Arnott

# Guitar man

She was unwinding after work
In her favourite bar
He was in the corner Playing his guitar
Soon her eyes locked with his
She imagined his kiss
But though he could play a thousand notes
He couldn't play the song
That her heart wrote
So soon her heart began to wander
He could hold her heart no longer
He could hold a thousand notes
But he couldn't play the song
That her heart wrote
And though his song burned on
In her heart
They never got the chance to start
So she finished her drink
And walked away
He still sits in the corner and plays
Another girl comes to the bar
And listens to him play guitar
Maybe he can play the notes
From the song that her heart wrote
Kim Arnott

# Hiding

I see you there
Hiding in the shadows
Head down
Not looking around
Or meeting anyone's eyes

I want to cry
You were the girl
Living each day
Going somewhere; feet bare
Face in the sun

I loved that girl
Now you mistrust
Never taking a stand; Or taking  anyone's hand
Hiding in the shadows
Kim Arnott

# Standing In the Shadows

Standing in the shadows
Where they first met the others eyes
After twenty two years
He said goodbye
Now she's standing in the shadows
Standing in the shadows
Trying not to cry

Standing in the shadows
As he walked away
After twenty two years
There is nothing left to say
Now she's standing in the shadows
Standing in the shadows
Wondering why

Standing in the shadows
Of what was once their home
After twenty two years
She is suddenly alone
Now she's standing in the shadows
Standing in the shadows

Wondering how she will get by

Standing in the shadows
Where it all began
After twenty two years
How can he be done
Now she's standing in the shadows
Standing in the shadows
Where he said goodbye

Standing in the shadows
It was the house where she was born
After twenty two years
It's the first time she's alone
Now she's standing in the shadows
Standing in the shadows
Wondering why

Standing in the shadows
Feeling the pain
After twenty two years
Some one has left her again
Now she's standing in the shadows
Standing in the shadows
Wishing she could cry

Standing in the shadows
In the place they first met

After twenty two years
How could he forget
 Now she's Standing in the shadows
Standing in the shadows
Letting out a sigh

She is standing in the shadows
Standing in the shadows
For another Goodbye
Kim Arnott

# The Meadow

So she took him to the meadow
Where she liked to go
To think; to sit and contemplate
The universe and everything in it

She wanted to walk
In this place that she loved
With him; and to talk
To share all the things that were special
To her
As they had been spending
A lot of time together

She wondered whether
They could share more
But he misunderstood
He thought he was doing; something good
To buy her the meadow
And to build on it a palace of gold

But gold costs a lot
As does land. She didn't understand
He was working so hard
He was always tired
She hardly saw him at all

When she did
He did not want to walk; talk or sit
She was lonely; and didn't enjoy
The palace of gold
It felt like a cage
Inside it's walls she missed him
And her meadow; Her poor fellow
Didn't understand why
She wrote a note saying goodbye
Hadn't he given her everything?
Yet she had chosen
To sit with some fool who gave her nothing
They would sit on a hill and chat
He had given her a palace of gold
Yet she had chosen that?
To sit on a hill and chat
Kim Arnott

# Believing

I am a hot singularity
Ready to explode
I could give you the universe
But you are unsure
Perhaps I am a dark star
Consuming all
I could be a void of nothingness
Or show you new worlds
I am the unknown
Ready to be explored

So! What will you do?
Accept me as a challenge
Will you try something new
Or take as fact; all that is flat
Laid out before you
On a map
I may be everything That could ever be
Or perhaps it is a trap
Kim Arnott

# B.d. Beautiful Dog

As I pick up my bag
Her tail starts to wag
It is time now; to head out  the door
Now covered in mud
Her head held so proud
She believes she's a Queen
I am sure

All the tears I have shed
On the top of her head
With her paws on my knees
How it comforts me
For when I look into her eyes
I can't tell any lies
So the talk it is free
How it comforts me

If there is a storm in the night
She gets quite a fright
As the wind it blows and it billows
She jumps up on my bed
Lies close to my head
With her eyes
Peaking out from under my pillows

All the tears I have shed
On the top of her head
With her paws on my knee's
How it comforts me
For when I look into her eyes
I can't tell any lies
How it comforts me

We take walks in the park
But when it gets dark
The lights from the cars
Start to worry her
She starts shaking so
I can't get her to go
The only thing I can do
Is to carry her

All the tears I have shed
On the top of her head
How it comforts me
For when I look into her eyes
I can't tell any lies
So the talk it is free
How it comforts me

I can not forget
That last trip to the vet
She watched as I picked up my bag
She was in such pain

And yet once again
I saw her tail
Start to wag

All the tears I have shed
On the top of her head
With her paws on my knee's
How it comforts me
For when I look into her eyes
I can't tell any lies
So the talk it is free
How it comforts me

Her memory is so warm
She still comforts me
Kim Arnott

# Universal

I looked; You smiled
Without a reason why
I took your hand
Thinking let's just give this a try
Then I felt the stars exploding
A spectacular Supa nova
I saw the universe
Unfolding in your eyes

So let's explore the earth
We are the miracle of birth
We belong here; you and me
All we have to do is be
We don't need; don't need
A reason why; to live; to be
To deserve to touch the sky

We need; but we don't need to do a thing
We are; we exist; we belong inside this ring
Of atmosphere; the reason we are here
We belong; it's our home; you and me
It is our place to be; all we have to do is be
We have all that we need
All we need to do is be
Take my hand; the universe is you and me
Kim Arnott

# Windows

She looked out of the window
To see what she could see
But the view was misty
So that she couldn't really see
It was then that she realised
That there were tears on her face
She wasn't looking outward
She was looking inward
Back to another time and place
Kim Arnott

# Leaving

There is an empty piece of ground
That lies between then and now
I have to get across it
But I am not sure That I know how

I used to feel so safe
In that place, we called our home
But when the door that trapped me ; opened
I had to walk through it on my own

The world isn't always sunshine
Sometimes no one can share your pain
But I would rather carry all the heavy stuff
Than be a prisoner once again
Kim Arnott

# The Ledge

On the ledge of indecision
I hear the eagles cry
There is a murmuring  of voices
People are down below
They pass by
I long to soar with the eagles
Through an endless sky
I could roam
But as I reach out for my freedom
Familiar voices call me home
Kim Arnott